Getting old is not for cowards

Getting old is not for cowards

Comfortable, healthy ageing

Jan Reed, Glenda Cook, Susan Childs and Amanda Hall

The **Joseph Rowntree Foundation** has supported this project as part of its programme of research and innovative development projects, which it hopes will be of value to policy makers, practitioners and service users. The facts presented and views expressed in this report are, however, those of the authors and not necessarily those of the Foundation.

Joseph Rowntree Foundation
The Homestead
40 Water End
York YO30 6WP
Website: www.jrf.org.uk

ISBN 1 85935 121 2   (paperback)
ISBN 1 85935 122 0   (pdf: available at www.jrf.org.uk)

A CIP catalogue record for this report is available from the British Library.

Cover design by Adkins Design

Prepared and printed by:
York Publishing Services Ltd
64 Hallfield Road
Layerthorpe
York
YO31 7ZQ
Tel: 01904 430033   Fax: 01904 430868   Website: www.yps-publishing.co.uk

Further copies of this report, or any other JRF publication, can be obtained either from the JRF website (www.jrf.org.uk/bookshop/) or from our distributor, York Publishing Services Ltd, at the above address.

CONTENTS

Acknowledgements   vi

1 Introduction   1

2 Stage one: background discussions   6
Focus groups and interviews   6
Interview themes and findings   8

3 Stage two: literature search and selection   23
Sources and types of material   23
Search strategy in this study   25
Selection of the literature for review   31
Results of the literature search   32

4 Stage three: literature reviewing   33
Organising framework   33

5 Conclusions   55

Bibliography   58

Appendix: Mapping of search terms across databases 67

ACKNOWLEDGEMENTS

This project was funded by the Joseph Rowntree Foundation. The study was carried out by two research centres, CCOP (Centre for Care of Older People) and IMRI (Information Management Research Institute), both based at Northumbria University. CCOP undertakes research that gives a voice to older people and has a commitment to multi-disciplinary research and to developing links with local agencies and organisations in statutory and non-statutory sectors. The research, development and consultancy activity of IMRI focuses on the people-centred aspects of the design, development and evaluation of information systems and services in a wide range of human and organisational contexts.

Members of the research team were:

- Professor Jan Reed and Glenda Cook, Centre for Care of Older People, Northumbria University

- Susan Childs and Amanda Hall, Information Management Research Institute, Northumbria University.

Key informants were older people from the following groups:

- members of a London-based leisure and educational voluntary group for the over-fifties

- attendees of a social services day centre

- residential home residents

- nursing home residents.

Scott Matthews of the NMAHP (Nursing, Midwifery and Allied Health Professionals) Research and Development Unit at Northumbria University acted as editorial adviser for the report.

1 INTRODUCTION

The project reported on here was commissioned by the Joseph Rowntree Foundation as a way of exploring different ideas about health for older people, alternatives to medical models that defined health simply as the absence of disease. In these medical models, with their emphasis on physiology and cure, growing old becomes a process of experiencing increasing deficits and problems, and the goals of intervention are to prevent or treat these problems. Much medical research and the resources to support it therefore concentrate on these deficits, and define 'healthy ageing' as avoiding or escaping them.

Partly in response to this deficit model, a movement has developed which seeks to promote the idea of growing older as a positive experience. This positive ageing movement has been developed with and by older people, but is exclusive in a different way. While the deficit model does not consider the needs of older people with few or no health problems, the positive ageing model focuses on these people to the exclusion of those who do have health problems. Positive images of older people engaged in heroic activities such as rock-climbing and wind-surfing, and displaying a determination not to 'give in' to ageing, may provide an alternative to deficit models of growing older (and, incidentally, represent a commercial opportunity for suppliers of anti-ageing drugs and holidays). However, they leave people who are not able or do not want to be heroic with little support or recognition.

Our title, *Growing Old is not for Cowards,* is taken from one of the interviews we did for this study, but in no way did the person who said this advocate a heroic model of growing old. Instead, her point was that growing older involves a number of difficulties and not a great deal of support, if you want to enjoy life. There is an argument, then, that significant research and debate should focus on these difficulties and the way in which they can impede enjoyment of life, and the support that older people need. The commissioning group felt that neither the deficit nor the heroic model necessarily reflected the views and experiences of older people, but that these models still tended to set research and policy agendas that would affect the lives of older people.

The question was asked in the commissioning brief, 'What matters to older people as they become older and less able to do things that they might have done in the past?' This question is an important one in a period where services and resources are being planned and reconfigured against a background of demographic change, where the proportion of older people in the population is growing. In addition, recent cultural and policy changes represent a move towards a more person-centred way of delivering services and support. The question 'what matters to older people?' then becomes fundamental for ensuring that services and support are relevant, appropriate and effective.

If services are based on ideas of health that have developed in professional and policy debates, then they run the risk of being, at best, irrelevant to the needs of older people and, at worst, dismissive of their views and damaging to them. Services that are designed to promote health for older people, therefore, need to take into account the ideas and wishes of older people themselves.

The commissioning brief also recognised that using the term 'older people' as a catch-all phrase fails to reflect the huge diversity among people in later life. Individuals differ in their aspirations and attitudes, as well as in their backgrounds, gender, class, ethnicity and health status. Any conclusions that are drawn, therefore, have to address this diversity, and any literature review would have to bear the limitations of sample or audience in mind.

The commissioning brief was wide-ranging: to examine the literature about what older people of different backgrounds and groups saw as health in later life, and what they thought would help them achieve this. As with other literature reviews, the objectives were to describe and evaluate knowledge, and to put together a picture of work that had been done that would form a basis for further research programmes and studies.

In keeping with the spirit of the commissioning process, we decided that the project should be reflective of, and shaped by, older people as well as researchers, bearing in mind the comment from Dorothy Jerrome:

> The methods used to acquire information are such that the subjective experience of ageing is subordinated to the objective accounts provided by youthful researchers. Very little contemporary research addresses the issues of ageing from the elderly person's point of view.
>
> (Jerrome, 1992, p. 4)

The study was therefore designed to include and respond to comments and ideas generated by older people. This is in contrast to the orthodox approach to literature review where key topics are located through processes of literature searching that have little to do with engagement with the world outside the library. The problem with such an approach, as we will argue, is that it tends to reflect the ideas and worldviews of the people who set up the systems for classifying and cataloguing material rather than those of the people examined in the literature itself.

This study comprises three stages: background discussions with older people, the generation of keywords and ideas used to find literature, and the analysis and review of the literature retrieved. However, the stages did not run consecutively. In stages two and three, use was made of 'background discussions' we were able to conduct with older people: to inform the choice of key words in stage two and to inform the analysis of the material we had acquired in stage three. Resources and timescales did not allow us to carry out an extensive exploration of older people's ideas, so the background discussion was restricted to small, easily accessible groups (see discussion of methodology in stage one). Even so, this limited data was extremely useful in shaping the literature search and the analysis.

Figure 1 shows the study represented diagrammatically.

Figure 1 The study represented diagrammatically

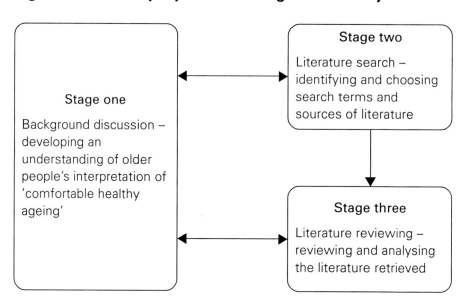

While the notion of 'stages' suggests a linear process, it is used here merely as a means of breaking down the research process into sections that are more comprehensible when described separately. By contrast, Figure 1 tries to capture the iterative character of the methodology employed in our research. The background discussions with older people were conducted concurrently with the literature search. Researchers held discussions with older people, brainstormed keywords, and revisited search strategies in the light of subsequent discussions. The discussions with older people then informed the framework for analysis and the results of those discussions were used to check subsequent interpretations of the literature. Comments made by older people were compared and contrasted with the research found in literature and our researchers were interested in identifying both the similarities and differences.

2 STAGE ONE: BACKGROUND DISCUSSIONS

Since the process of searching databases involves using specific search terms and keywords, we decided to begin the process by trying to generate such terms from conversations with older people.

Focus groups and interviews

The group and individual interviews covered the following topics.

- Meanings of being healthy.

- What does the term 'comfortable healthy living' in later life mean?

- Is there a difference between 'comfortable healthy ageing' and 'healthy ageing'?

- How do older people maintain an active healthy life or 'comfortable healthy ageing'?

- What helps older people to achieve 'healthy ageing'/ 'comfortable healthy ageing'?

The sampling strategy for the interviews actively sought to recruit older people with different physical abilities, and who were receiving different levels of personal and health-care support. This provided the opportunity to capture the views of a diverse rather than a homogenous group of people, whose perceptions of health may differ. Twenty-two older people, 17 women and five men, participated in the following interviews.

- Two group interviews were carried out with older people who were members of a leisure and educational voluntary group for those over 50 ($n = 10$; the average age of these participants was 74).

- One group interview was held with four older people who attended a social services day centre.

- One group interview was held with six older people living in a residential care home.

- Two individual interviews were carried out with nursing home residents. One of these individuals experienced expressive dysphasia following a stroke, and she required a quiet setting and the opportunity to take her time to answer questions and to present her views. The other interviewee had hearing problems and was unable to take part in group discussion.

These interviews were tape-recorded and transcribed verbatim. Standard methods of open-coding were used to analyse this data, to identify the ideas that the participants held about their health and what was important to them. The process of data collection and the findings arising from analysis of this data served four purposes. First, the discussions with the participants were instrumental in developing ideas about keywords and search terms that were used to locate literature of relevance to the brief. Second, the findings were used as criteria for selecting relevant items to review. Third, the findings contributed to the development of a framework to organise the literature that was retrieved. Fourth, the findings were also used to check whether gaps existed in the literature that was retrieved from the electronic databases and from the grey literature search, to prompt further searches.

Interview themes and findings

The interview transcripts were first analysed to identify themes and topics. The following discussion itemises and expands on these.

What do older people understand by the term 'comfortable healthy ageing'?

Diverse views were held about the meaning conveyed by the term 'comfortable healthy ageing'. Some participants suggested that it implied acceptance of one's circumstances or making adjustments to changing personal circumstances:

> I think of comfortable in many ways ... whatever your problems are, you can become comfortable with them. It's an adjustment to life.

Such views corresponded with dictionary definitions of the word 'comfortable' of 'being at ease' or 'to make comfortable'. Others argued that the phrase 'comfortable healthy ageing' was associated with ideas of optimum physical health. This meaning was closely associated with definitions of comfortable as 'a state of physical well-being' and being 'free from discomfort'. To these older people, this way of thinking about comfortable healthy ageing was linked to the understandings that they held of healthy ageing, which suggested a disease-free state and experiencing optimal physical health. This was an ideal state that all of the participants desired; however, the daily reality of decreasing stamina, aches and pains, and coping with illness and disability led them to conclude that 'healthy ageing' was a term that did not represent their experience of later life.

Finally, some participants indicated that the expression 'comfortable healthy ageing' held meanings of financial and material well-being for them:

> Comfortable healthy ageing, no money worries – which a lot of pensioners will have. And that is not comfortable.

> Comfortable to me would be having double the pension I had. Then I could afford to spend something to treat myself, instead of only just having enough money to survive, to pay the phone bill or to pay the electric and to pay the rent.

> And so the term comfortable ... I personally don't like it because it is ... a material thing.

These views are analogous to definitions of comfortable as 'physical things that make life more comfortable' and 'having an adequate standard of living' (Collins English Dictionary, 1999). Hence, different people ascribed different meanings to the expression 'comfortable healthy ageing' and the meanings that individuals held were focused on a particular facet of their life.

This range of meanings led to discussions about other terms that they said reflected their varied experiences:

- experiencing well-being

- fulfilled later life

- enjoyable later life

- a satisfying later life.

Health was, therefore, a multi-dimensional concept that included physical, mental, functional, social, spiritual and material/financial aspects. The interviewees' concept of health, therefore, was more than a process of adaptation to the changing circumstances of their ageing body, or the mere presence or absence of disease or discomfort, or the experience of material well-being. Health was defined as being able to establish and maintain a sense of ease and enjoyment in their lives, by identifying and reaching their own personal goals. A number of components were identified as instrumental to shaping health: physical condition, adapting to continuous physical change, functional abilities, relationships, maintaining independence, financial satisfaction, fulfilling personal objectives, pursuing interests and taking part in meaningful activity. The participants' discussions of these components are presented in detail in the following sections.

Later life: a time of changes in physical condition and functional abilities

Later life was presented as a time when the body is continuously changing. These changes, as described by the older people in the study, often reflected a deficit model of growing older. The majority of interviewees had experienced decreased stamina, a general slowing down and generalised aches and pains:

Getting old is not for cowards.

Yes.

Yeah!

Well you need to be courageous to get old because you do get aches and pains and illness and all sorts of things … but to have that courage you need to interact with other people and that is very important.

These changes were associated with the ageing process, and were distinguished from pathological changes resulting from illness and disease. The following discussion illustrates how the participants accepted that the changes that they experienced were an inevitable part of normal ageing and they adjusted their activities to accommodate this:

I think when you get older you have to pace yourself you know you … you must realise that you can't physically do what you could do when you were younger, and you pace yourself.

Well your body helps you doesn't it?

Yeah! Well your body tells you to do that, but some people don't do that. I … and I think it's very important to pace yourself.

If I go at the same speed that I used to go at I would be out of breath.

Those who experienced relatively good physical health discussed how they took active measures to engage in a range of activities with the aim of maintaining their existing level of health and preventing illness and disease. They planned a regular exercise schedule that was not too strenuous, ensured that they had a well-balanced diet and complied with the health advice that they were aware of. Their physical health was very important to them and they were aware that, if their physical health deteriorated, they would no longer be able to pursue their life as they wished.

The very active and physically healthy participants stressed that they were aware that the probability of experiencing physical decline was high. They acknowledged that their circumstances might change and began to prepare for this by developing new interests that required use of different abilities to enable them to continue to experience fulfilment in advanced old age:

> If perhaps you had got arthritis or the physical problems in older age, there are still very many things that you can participate in mentally.

When the physical condition deteriorates

Many of the interviewees, however, experienced chronic ill health and disability. Some spoke of the frustrations that they experienced when they could no longer do what they wanted to do:

> Yes! Yes! Yes! That is old age isn't it? That's old age. You would like to do something but can't because you are not able to.

They felt restricted as they made adjustments to their life in ways that they did not desire. Some conveyed their dissatisfaction with their life, whereas others indicated that they accepted that they had physical problems and emphasised their capacity to enjoy life in ways that were not dependent on their physical abilities:

> I think that's why we enjoy coming in here [to the day centre]. We're all elderly. We're all disabled in one way or the other and we enjoy each other's company because you don't have to keep explaining, 'Oh I've got this, I'm going blind' and ... you don't have to go through that.

> It's very rarely spoken at our table, health. Is it?

> No.

> Nobody talks about it.

> We all know each other's problems but nobody at the table talks about it.

> No, well ...

> We all know we're ill but we can enjoy ourselves.

These older people were highly dependent on others to assist them to meet all of their personal needs and they acknowledged that their physical abilities were limited. They were also conscious of what they could do and spoke of how they embraced every day to gain the maximum pleasure by focusing on what they could rather than on what they could not do. They spoke of the importance of 'having a positive attitude amidst trying circumstances' and the need to make psychological adjustments as physical abilities change in later life. They expressed the view

13

that experiencing physical problems did not necessarily mean that the individual was unhealthy – it was possible to experience mental well-being and to continue to engage in a meaningful social life when physical abilities declined.

Engaging in relationships

Interacting with other people was viewed as extremely important to maintain and improve health in later life. To these older people, maintaining contact with family promoted a sense of continuity throughout their life span and across the generations; however, this was often problematic. Frequently, family members did not live nearby and, as their physical health deteriorated, travelling became increasingly difficult. Many spoke of the importance of the telephone as a way to keep in touch:

> My young ones phone, they're not writers but the oldest daughter, we write to each other. Every week we write to each other telling the goings on you know what's going on up in Aberdeen because I've got eight grandchildren and eight great-grandchildren. So there's plenty going up there. But there again, they want me to go up there but I just cannot travel on my own now. It's too much.

In contrast to family relationships, the participants highlighted the importance of maintaining and developing relationships that were based on mutual interests and need. They argued that sharing and enjoying experiences with others had a positive impact on their health:

> I think, really, that people keep healthier by going out to groups. I certainly do.

Yes! We do have fun. We have a good laugh.

Yes! As we did yesterday afternoon, for example. We shared you know …

We had a little singsong you know … it's fun.

I go to an exercise class and a fitness place in here for … for the senior citizen. And I find the class motivates me to keep going … if I hadn't the group, I would not go for the exercise, but I have the group and I know all the group who turn up, and I have a chat with this one today and that one, and that one, and that one … and I have a cup of tea afterwards. The groups do motivate the people … it makes you come out.

It was not always possible to maintain friendships in later life because changes in personal circumstances such as retirement and ill health were disruptive; therefore, there was much discussion about developing skills, and creating and taking opportunities to forge new friendships. This was difficult for those who lacked confidence to meet with strangers, or lived in circumstances where there were limited opportunities to meet others with similar interests (for example, those who were housebound as a consequence of physical disability). The interviewees particularly valued groups (i.e. leisure and activity groups) and services (i.e. day centres, residential care) that created socialising opportunities because this enabled them to regain a dimension in their life that they missed and had enjoyed:

It sounds silly but it's true. I had a very, very bad turn a few years, I had a very, very bad heart attack and it took me seven months to get out the front door because it was like … oh I'll fall. That was a terrible time and then I got in here and met everybody, made friends easy and I've just taken it from there but I still only come out Tuesday and a Thursday and on a Sunday obviously I'm at the family's but these two days are important to me.

Maintaining independence and taking risks

Living an independent life was highly valued as this enabled individuals to live their life as they desired, and some of the discussions we had reflected aspects of heroic ageing models. For example, some strongly refused to 'give in' to growing older and to see it as a time of inevitably increasing dependence. They argued, however, that a balance had to be maintained between living an independent life and interdependence with those who provided help and support to meet the demands of day-to-day life. Though they appreciated the support of others, they strived to maintain control over their lives:

> Well, I have had a couple of serious operations and, as luck would have it, I have had someone to look after me [following discharge from hospital]. I realised that, while I can do things for myself, I want to be able to do that …if you don't live with your family you are enclosed by it. This is not some detrimental thing, they might be lovely people but they have got their way of going on and it's not yours. And you don't want to be enclosed in their way of living because that is a loss of independence. So you want to stay as independent for as long as possible whatever that means to you.

For those living in their own homes, it was possible to experience a degree of independence even in circumstances where the older person was highly dependent on others to assist them in every aspect of their daily lives. Those living in residential accommodation were more acutely aware of their limited independence and the restrictions that they faced by living in a communal environment. Some did, however, discuss how they were involved in decisions about their lives and they were supported to carry them out by the staff in the home and this led to a more satisfying outcome.

The interviewees spoke of the importance of making their own choices and acting on those choices, even if this involved a degree of risk-taking. Decisions that involved evaluation of different outcomes had the potential to lead to conflict between the older person and their family and carers when they all attached greater value to different outcomes. This is illustrated in the following extract that focuses on the way that the older person's view of the risks of using a motorised scooter differed from the views that her daughter held:

My children weren't happy about me getting a scooter. They said: 'You're not able to control it'. I said 'I can and in my time I will be', and I got the scooter. I paid the bill over three years but it's mine and I get out and about. The dog and I go for lunch all over ... I had to make the push to get myself outside the door, although this daughter is not happy about me on the scooter. I sometimes have to go where traffic is and ...

That would terrify me.

It does when I go across the M1 ... there are big lorries and everything and I'm waiting for somebody to knock the back of my scooter. They don't stop. They stop for other traffic but they don't stop for the scooter ... I was without it last year ... A car mounted the pavement and smashed me into a step ... I was so shaken, you know. It was very frightening but it had nothing to do with me. My daughter said to me ... 'that's the kind of thing that can happen' but I said it wasn't my fault: I was on the pavement and he mounted the pavement and made me crash.

This woman was aware of the potential harms that she faced when using the scooter; however, she argued that she assigned greater value to other outcomes. By using the scooter, her social life and independence were enhanced and she was presented with new possibilities and different ways to enjoy her life:

I spent four years in the house and when I got my scooter I met people that I hadn't seen for years. They were shocked because they thought I'd died.

Having adequate money

This was an important issue, which was spontaneously discussed in every interview, perhaps in response to the association of financial satisfaction with ideas of being comfortable. There was a consensus that having adequate money referred to the monetary resources to fund everyday needs, and the range of activities that led to enjoyment and satisfaction in later life. Many of the interviewees lived on low incomes and they described their lives as 'living on the breadline'. They had to make decisions about buying fresh, nutritious food or purchasing 'out-of-date and poor quality food'. While decisions about buying poor quality food enabled them to take part in inexpensive activities or to put a little money aside for repairs to their home that may arise in the future, they were also aware that such decisions had a negative impact on their health. They also spoke of not being able to budget for new clothing and having to request clothing as gifts or to shop at second-hand shops if the need arose. Living in these circumstances was viewed as a harsh existence contributing to much 'stress and worry'.

In contrast to this, some of the interviewees had incomes and access to assets that enabled them to make choices and to fulfil those choices. They had the monetary resources to live their life as they desired and this contributed to a sense of control over their circumstances. This was particularly discussed with reference to being able to pay for specialised diets, equipment, aids and adaptations to the home, substitute care, and assistance to maintain their home to enable them to cope with the effects of illness and declining physical abilities.

Having money provided options, even in circumstances where the older person required long-term care and support in meeting every aspect of their personal needs. They had the choice of paying for additional care, when the ceiling for a care package was reached, and remaining in their own home or moving to a care home. Those with limited or no monetary resources did not have different options when they were in these circumstances, and they faced the prospect of giving up their home and moving to care.

To these older people, having enough money was valued because it provided the means to do what they wanted to do. With money, it was possible to maintain relationships, retain some degree of independent living, pursue interests, experience financial security and have a sense of control over one's circumstances.

Fulfilling desires and personal objectives

Following a lifetime of work and/or family commitments, later life was viewed as a time to 'do the things that you always wanted to do'. Those who experienced good physical health were able to identify the opportunities for leisure and learning that were

19

available to them and they were able to fulfil personal aspirations. They attempted to do this while they experienced good health, as they were aware that opportunities to do this would reduce as physical abilities deteriorated. Those with limited physical abilities found that their personal objectives changed as their life circumstances altered and they experienced fulfilment as they attained the goals that they had set for themselves.

Keeping busy by taking part in meaningful activity

A full and enjoyable life was associated with keeping busy, and this was a theme that all of the participants constantly referred to. They spoke of the various leisure activities that filled their days and emphasised that each activity had an inherent value as it enabled them to fulfil a personal need. Through their activities, they were able to pursue their interests, and develop new skills and knowledge. Engaging in activities created opportunities to meet others with similar interests and develop new friendships, whereas physical activity was viewed as particularly important to promote physical health. Other activities that required reasoning, problem solving and use of memory were important to 'keep the grey cells going'. Pursuits such as watching the TV and reading newspapers were necessary to enable the older person to keep in touch with the wider community that they lived in. All of these activities mattered to those taking part in the interviews as a way of achieving goals that were important to them.

In addition to taking part in leisure activities, the participants discussed their membership of different types of groups, such as residents' associations, day centres and voluntary organisations. Their contribution to these groups was important as it enabled them to feel that they were able to make a valued contribution to the community that they were part of. This was important because the process of becoming a pensioner had been a negative experience for many of the interviewees and had eroded their self-esteem:

> I think that when you retire all of a sudden from being a worker, a commuter, somebody who does the shopping … You retire and you are at home and you are nothing. You have no sense of belonging whatsoever.

In contrast, taking part in meaningful activity had a positive impact on the way that they regarded themselves:

> If you work it gives you the satisfaction in knowing that you are wanted.

> You belong to the community, you belong to a part of something.

Being able to take part in meaningful activity was dependent on many factors. While the individual's physical and mental abilities can restrict or enhance what they can do, what is available and accessible locally is also extremely important. Features of the environment and community such as inaccessible buildings, limited public transport, lack of support from able-bodied people and the attitudes of others were mentioned in the discussions:

> I mean I'd go to our church but there isn't a ramp.

> As I say, we used to go the disabled club, but that packed up through no able-bodied people there to help the disabled. You know, although we're a disabled club, we need able-bodied people to put out the tea and to help

with lots of different things, you know, and it just isn't there and it was great. It was every fortnight and it just broke your week up. I don't see my friends now and we have lost touch with each other.

Interdependence of the components of health

Analysis of the data showed that there were connections between the components and that they were interdependent. The things that people do are dependent on their willingness to take part in activities, their physical and mental abilities, and the material and financial means to provide the resources to do what they want to do. When all of the components that were discussed above were present, the interviewees suggested that their experience of health was positively affected or negatively so when any component was lacking. While this is the case, it is important to point to the way that the different components were used to mediate the effects of deficiencies in others. This was particularly illustrated through the discussion of having enough money to purchase aids and equipment or to fund adaptations to the home when physical abilities decline.

To these older people, 'health' referred to more than physical condition. However, physical abilities were extremely important in enabling them to do what they wanted to do. When physical abilities declined, adjusting to new circumstances and doing other meaningful things enabled these older people to experience a fulfilled or a satisfying existence. The models of health that were expressed in these background discussions were different to either the deficit or the heroic models found in the media and elsewhere. The participants did not see older age as a time of inevitable decline but, when decline did happen, they adjusted to it and developed strategies to ensure that they could still do what was important to them.

3 STAGE TWO: LITERATURE SEARCH AND SELECTION

The second stage involved searching the literature, informed by the conversations and discussions held with older people, and by previous reading and work in the area. This stage had two elements to it: first, the retrieval of material from electronic databases to form a list of papers and items and, second, the selection of relevant items for acquisition (copies obtained through inter-library loans or electronic journals). Uncovering relevant material through searching literature is not a straightforward activity, however. Between authors writing material and its inclusion in a database there is a complex process whereby, at each stage, decisions are made about what an item is about.

Sources and types of material

There are issues about what is published and how it is made available to potential readers. Academic and professional literature is usually published in an organised way through journals, books, reports of conferences, etc. These items are managed by commercial publishers who ensure that potential readers can gain access to this literature. They achieve this by labelling each item with full bibliographic information, thus making it available for purchase and distributing and promoting it to database producers.

Databases are commercially developed for specific audiences or markets. They are often specialised, including material from only a limited number of journals that have established records of containing relevant material of a suitable quality. When an item is included in a database, keywords or search terms are assigned. This means that they can be searched under author, title, date, or subject headings (keywords) depending on the database and its structure.

All these processes take time. It can take many months, or even years, before a written article is actually published in a journal. It can then take a similar period of time before an article appears in a database, if it ever does. Databases will therefore not necessarily contain the most up-to-date material.

There is another type of literature, 'grey literature', which is not necessarily attainable through conventional publication and retrieval systems. However, such literature can often contain very useful information, particularly about projects and services provided by individual organisations and research projects or in specific localities. It consists of locally produced reports, meeting papers, discussion and policy documents, etc.

Grey literature can be variable in the bibliographic details items are given. Some may be described fully, while others might lack an author's name or even a date, and it can be unclear who the publisher is (i.e. which organisation has produced it). Grey literature is not recorded in databases, nor is it peer-reviewed. Usually, the author and producer do not take even the simple step of depositing their work with the British Library (BL) to ensure its appearance in the BL catalogue and availability through inter-library loan. The normal method of publication of grey literature is the in-house production of a small number of copies that are sent to a restricted list of people. The content of the literature could be confidential or organisationally sensitive, which will restrict the initial audience even further. A wider, or future, audience is not catered for.

Search strategy in this study

The process of searching and locating items involves negotiating all the complexities discussed above. It also involves understanding the limitations of databases, the way that they use search terms and the material they index. It also involves understanding the environment in which research and development takes place, in that research gets funding only if it fits in with funders' priorities and goals, and their model of the world. Medical research funders would therefore fund research that accords with their priorities and uses terms that fit with their language. In this respect, they operate in the same way as social scientific research funders. Since older people are not usually funders of research, and are only just beginning to have a say in research priorities, it is not surprising that the search terms and keywords in databases may not fit their models of knowledge.

The process of identifying and selecting items to fit the project brief, therefore, involves processes of translation and interpretation backed up by an understanding of the way in which information becomes available, and ways in which it can be accessed. The terms of the project brief had to be interpreted in the light of database search terms and author keywords. This process relied on the knowledge that the research team had of literature searching and of the topic being explored. From this, it was possible to make judgements about the relevance of material and also to generate items for inclusion in the review based on the researcher's expertise in this area.

The subject of the brief 'comfortable healthy ageing' uses concepts that are difficult to describe precisely, and additionally uses words and phrases that have general, wide-ranging usage. If you are looking for keywords to describe older people, there are many available, including 'older'/'old', 'ageing'/'aged', 'elderly', 'retired', 'senior' (linked with 'people'/'person'/'citizen'),

25

'geriatrics', 'pensioners'. The availability of keywords for health-related matters is also diverse, including 'optimal', 'positive' and 'healthy ageing' as a few examples. These words then have to be combined together in a meaningful way to create a final, full-search strategy. Often, when terms like these are used in searches, items are found that are wholly irrelevant to the project topic. This is because these common words are, of course, used to mean different things in different contexts. For example, 'aged expectant mothers' (who are pregnant but older than in their early twenties) and a 'healthy pregnancy' combine the words 'aged' and 'healthy' in an entirely different context. Such irrelevant items are often called 'false hits'.

In searching, there is always a balance between getting relevant items and avoiding irrelevant items. If you aim for a precise, specific search, you will retrieve less irrelevant items, but with the downside that you will have excluded relevant items in the process. If you go for a sensitive search, to try and retrieve as many relevant items as possible, then the downside is that you will also retrieve many irrelevant items too. One point to remember is that, for the many reasons discussed above, even the most sensitive search will never find all the relevant items that exist in the database being searched.

A different search process was needed for grey literature, as databases, on the whole, cannot be used. Traditional (non-electronic) methods are appropriate here, for example, looking in the reference lists of articles and books to see what information sources the authors used, which could include grey literature as well as academic literature; asking experts in the topic for their recommendations of grey literature. These traditional methods can be powerful approaches and find very useful information, but they are clearly only scratching at the surface of the grey literature that must exist. Traditional methods are also useful in searching for academic literature to fill some of the gaps in coverage that will always occur in a literature search. They form part of the procedures for undertaking a systematic review too (see later definition).

Our approach was to go for a more sensitive search and accept that we would retrieve a number of irrelevant as well as relevant items. The results of a pilot search are given in the Appendix, which shows how large a number of items were initially retrieved. We dealt with these by a step-wise selection process whereby two members of the project team looked at the results independently, then compared their choice and came to an agreement through discussion. For the first stage, the obvious 'false hits' were discarded. In the second stage, less obvious irrelevant items were discarded, for example, those that, on more detailed reading, were irrelevant, or those that, though broadly in the topic area, did not meet the specific requirements of the project brief.

A final point will set the literature review for this project in context with other literature reviews. In the health field, there is a growing use of systematic reviews of the literature. These use detailed procedures that aim for a more comprehensive and objective search and selection of the literature (NHS CRD, 2001). However, systematic reviews are very costly in terms of money and staff time; they can cost tens of thousands of pounds and can take up to a year or more to complete, with a person being involved full-time and with other staff on a part-time basis.

The literature search was focused on published material and did not involve substantial amounts of grey literature. This was because grey literature tends to be organisational rather than conceptual; it is mainly about practical issues, such as development evaluation. The grey literature that was accessed for this study was largely, therefore, that found on websites and newsletters, and was not explicitly about models of health, although these were implied by the content and the way in which the material was presented.

The process of literature searching is shown in the following box.

Literature searching and selection

Identifying literature

- Project team brainstorm of search terms and initial search from selected databases conducted.
- Calls placed on electronic mailing lists to request research in progress or research reports.
- Websites of key organisations in the field of ageing were checked for relevant research reports.

Selecting the literature

- Duplicate references and false hits removed.
- Selection of literature that reflected the themes that were identified from analysis of the interviews.

Identifying further literature

- Hand searching of current journals for material relating to older people's relationships and social networks.

Searches were carried out on the following databases:

- AMED (Allied and Complementary Medicine)

- CINAHL (Nursing and Allied Health)

- EBM Reviews – Cochrane Controlled Trials Register

- Cochrane Reviews.

(Note: Medline was not used as the large number of hits retrieved made searching within the project constraints unfeasible.)

Two search strategies were employed.

The initial search strategy retrieved any English language articles that contained terms (one or more) from all three of the lists below. The following lists were designed to capture the concepts of 'older people', 'healthy' and 'perceptions', respectively:

- 'older people', 'elderly people', 'geriatric(s)', 'retired', 'retirement', 'senior citizen(s)', 'pensioner(s)' (all used to capture the concept of 'older people')

- 'healthy', 'well-being', 'wellness', 'quality of life', 'happiness' (all used to capture the concept of 'healthy')

- 'belief(s)', 'model(s)', 'definition(s)', 'perception(s)', 'meaning(s)'.

The subsequent strategy retrieved items that had any of the following phrases (designed to capture the concept of 'healthy ageing'):

- 'healthy ageing' ('aging'), 'active ageing' ('aging'), 'successful ageing' ('aging'), 'comfortable ageing' ('aging'), 'optimal ageing' ('aging'), 'positive ageing' ('aging'), 'healthy longevity', 'healthy and productive ageing' ('aging'), 'healthy life style'.

The results of the two search strategies were combined and duplicated items were removed. This resulted in 996 references.

While searches were being undertaken through the above databases, websites of key organisations in the field of ageing (such as Age Concern and Help the Aged) were checked for relevant research reports. Policy documents were identified and appropriate ones selected for review. However, in some cases, older documents were not available on the websites. Additionally, there were information leaflets/books geared to older people themselves. These were not selected for review. In any case, this approach did not identify research material.

Calls were placed on organisational mailing lists to request research in progress or research reports. This resulted in some authors of PhD studies offering us excerpts from their theses. While these were of excellent quality, they were not used in the analysis, as it was decided that their scope did not match the remit of the study.

Hand searching

Following identification of the literature from the initial search and analysis of the interview data, it was found that themes (family relationships, social networks and adapting to changing circumstances) that were emphasised by the interviewees were not evident in the literature that had been located. A subsequent hand search of the following journals was carried out to expand the literature search within the limited timescale of the project:

- *Ageing and Society*

- *Aging and Mental Health.*

This search retrieved any English language articles published after 1997 that contained terms (one or more) from both of the lists below. The two lists were designed to capture the concepts of 'older people' and 'social relationships':

- 'older people', 'elderly people', 'geriatric(s)', 'retired', 'retirement', 'senior citizen(s)', 'pensioner(s)'

- 'social networks', 'relationships', 'friendships', 'social isolation', 'loneliness'.

Thirteen articles were identified and retrieved through this process.

Selection of the literature for review

Following the identification or retrieval of items through search procedures, a process of selection had to take place to weed out irrelevant or duplicated material. It is difficult with such a topic to use terms that are precise and unique, and would result in retrieval of only the required articles from the online database searches. Inevitably, a large number of false hits were obtained and these had to be discarded by hand. To do this, the full computer record of each identified item (bibliographic details, abstract and keywords) was read independently by two members of the project team. Nine-hundred-and-ninety-six items had been identified in the database searches and 13 through hand searching. The hand-searching process, however, incorporates selection, so these references were included in the final number for review.

Items were selected for review if they addressed one or more themes that had been discussed by the interviewees. These were difficult judgements because the computer records varied in quality, some giving a detailed account of the content of the article whereas others provided scanty information. In the latter situation, the items were submitted for retrieval and a decision to discard or include it was based on reading of the full article. The team members then met to discuss their selections and reached a consensus regarding the final selection, which comprised 66 items from the computer search (see Bibliography). Full-text versions of these articles were obtained for review, as were the 13 located through hand searching and one item from the web search (66 + 13 +1 = 80).

Results of the literature search

The various stages above resulted in the selection of 80 references for review. In addition, the research team identified items from their own reading that were relevant to this project. In total, 115 references were reviewed. In the following chapter, we present this review but, in the interests of simplicity and brevity, we have not directly referred to all of this material. Full details of all of the references are included in either the reference list (material referenced in the text) or the further reading list (material used to inform the discussion) in the Bibliography.

4 STAGE THREE: LITERATURE REVIEWING

The third stage of the project consisted of obtaining and reviewing the literature we had identified in stage two. Reading the final selected papers resulted in another process of sorting, or making sense of, the material. While the search terms that had identified the papers provided an indication of their topic area, reading them showed that their content, ideas, frameworks and findings were more complex than the very simple and crude search terms that had been used. This meant that analysing the material according to search terms ran the risk of over-simplifying the work, and missing out on some interesting and challenging ideas that the work explored.

Organising framework

In all of this complexity, it was necessary to use some sort of framework for organising the material, so that it became manageable and could be summarised coherently. This framework would need to include all of the material, and show the relationships between different research strands and debates, without becoming so complex that the overall shape of the literature would be obscured. There are accepted processes (meta-analysis techniques) for summarising literature which is experimental, and which allows findings of studies to be combined, but these depend on the material being very similar in methods, goals and presentation. These techniques were not appropriate with this material, which was very diverse. The goal was to capture this diversity and range, rather than develop uniform conclusions. Choosing a framework, however, needed to be a process that did not impose a researcher-driven order on the material. In other words, it needed to reflect the views and ideas of older people.

The process was therefore informed and shaped by the focus group material that we had collected, and the themes that we had identified in this. However, we were also helped by the work, with older people, of Lucinda L. Bryant, Kitty K. Corbett and Jean S. Kutner, exploring their views and definitions of healthy ageing (Bryant *et al.*, 2001). Since the model that this team developed reflected our own focus group material, we decided to use it as a framework for organising and analysing the material. Henceforth, we shall refer to the model as the 'Bryant model' and to the study that created it as the 'Bryant study'.

In essence, the Bryant model specifies that healthy ageing is a matter of being able to 'go and do something meaningful'. Much of the focus group data echoed this idea, as people talked about their priorities, their values and their satisfactions, the strategies they had been able to use to achieve these and the obstacles that they saw lying in their way. The components of the Bryant model are as follows.

- First, people have to have the *ability* to go and do something, which includes physical abilities. Physical function, according to the Bryant model, is a basis for independence and, conversely, maintaining independence is one way of evaluating physical ability. In other words, the Bryant study evaluated older people's physical abilities in terms of how independent they were able to be in doing certain things.

- People also have to have the *resources* to go and do something, and the Bryant model includes friends and family as social resources, alongside access to health services. The Bryant model does not include financial resources, presumably because the respondents in their study did not mention money. In our work, however, money was discussed in the focus groups, and was a feature of the articles and papers identified, and so the model has been extended to include this. Our discussion of resources therefore draws on Arber and Ginn's notion of a 'resource triangle', where material resources (including housing, possessions and income), caring resources (including support from family and friends) and health resources (including physical abilities) make up the three points of the triangle (Arber and Ginn, 1991).

- The Bryant model also points to the willingness 'to go and do something', which they term 'attitude'. Again, we have extended this notion to incorporate the range of individual and personal perspectives that were found in the literature, and termed *personal outlooks*. The Bryant study goes beyond the narrow term 'attitude' to discuss sense of self, sense of control and focus on others, as ways in which their respondents explained how some people can describe themselves as healthy even with serious physical problems. In our study, the term 'personal outlook' has been used to include the literature and focus group data on individual views on quality of life, sense of self-efficacy and sense of autonomy and control.

- One of the key elements of the Bryant model is, of course, *having something meaningful to do*. This idea is not just about the availability of activities, but also involves a discussion of what is meaningful to people. In this category, then, we have included literature about meaning in later life, and about the satisfactions and achievements that are linked to this.

Some caveats must be made about the use of the Bryant model. First, there may have been other suitable models, or the research team could have developed their own. The Bryant model does, however, meet some of the requirements of the study. It was developed with older people and it reflected our data, both from the focus groups and from the literature search. In a study with limited time and resources, the development of a new model was not feasible, and the literature search had not located any other models developed with older people. Therefore, the Bryant model was chosen, with the provisos that it would serve as a starting point for thinking, and that it would be expanded and developed as necessary to reflect the material that we had.

In the second place, the Bryant model had been developed from a research study that had interviewed older people identified as rating their health differently than would be expected from their response to a health status questionnaire. Either they rated their health as better or worse than would be expected from their questionnaire response. The remit of the Bryant study was therefore to explore these discrepancies and move towards an understanding of dimensions of health that go beyond the absence of disease. This literature review, therefore, had a different remit and focus, which means that the Bryant model could not be expected to fit perfectly without some modification, as noted above.

Abilities

One of the factors that the Bryant model identifies as leading to perceptions of health is the extent to which people have the ability to 'go and do something meaningful'. While abilities are not exclusively physical, and mental alertness is important, physical abilities are a prerequisite for many activities. Aside from the limitations imposed by illness and its treatment, there are limitations resulting from decreased mobility, hearing and eyesight problems, and other problems in function, which make going and doing more difficult.

There is a body of literature, derived from surveys and censuses, which shows the incidence of health and functional problems experienced by older people. Some of this is from official surveys, such as the Health Survey for England 2000 (2002), which involve large sample sizes. In some ways, the size of a survey can lead to problems with the data it collects. The pressure to collect and analyse a lot of responses means that questions have to be very structured and unambiguous – a requirement that does not do justice to grey areas or differences in subjective views. What surveys usually focus on is measurable, observable facts, such as the number of visits to a GP or medications taken, rather than subjective feelings and definitions of wellness or illness. As Heathcote (2000) has described, these researcher-derived concerns also manifest themselves in attempts to classify older people as being 'young-old' and 'old-old'. Other possibilities for sub-categorisation are suggested by a typology of health problem, gender, social class and other factors. In these ways, the heterogeneity of older people is made more 'manageable' for research purposes. Heathcote's comments that these were derived partly from medical models of health and disease have potentially wider implications. The essential point is that researchers can come to research with worldviews that come from their background and training, rather than from the experiences of older people.

Further complications and ambiguities are introduced by the different terms used to describe survey results and the ways that these can be used differently by different authors, and by the general population. The World Health Organisation has proposed the following definitions:

- *impairment*: a 'loss or abnormality of psychological, physiological or anatomical structure or function'

- *disability*: a 'restriction or lack of ability to perform an activity in a manner or within a range considered normal for a human being'

- *handicap*: a 'disadvantage for a given individual, resulting from an impairment or disability, that limits or prevents the fulfilment of a role (depending on age, sex and social and cultural factors) for that individual'.

Using these definitions, the Health Survey for England 2000 (2002) discussed the complex relationship between ageing, health, disease and ability. The report pointed to the association between growing older and physiological changes that may limit activity that could be classed as impairments. If these impairments further restricted function, they could lead to disability and could eventually result in handicap. There is thus a complex relationship between normal human ageing processes and the effects that they have, aside from any disease or illness processes.

What the Health Survey found was that, among men in private households, the proportion reporting disability was 35 per cent among men aged 65–79 and 62 per cent among those aged 80 and over. Comparable figures for women were 35 per cent and 64 per cent. These figures do not include people in care homes, where the reported levels of disability were higher – with less difference between the age groups. People in care homes also had more severe disabilities and a higher incidence of locomotor disability. The survey also found that many people had a combination of disabilities and that the incidence of multiple disability increased with age. The causes of disability reported in the survey were mainly arthritis and cardiovascular problems. There was also data that indicated that disability was linked to gender and class – that women were more likely to report disability than men and that people from manual occupations reported more disability than those who had had office or white-collar jobs.

These figures seem to support deficit models of ageing – that it is a process of decline. Other data, however, suggest that increases in physical problems do not necessarily result in lower self-ratings of health. The survey also asked people to give an overall rating of their health, which provides some interesting data, which suggests that the presence of a disability and perceived health are not always connected. Fifty-eight per cent of men and 59 per cent of women living in private households described their health as good, and only 13 per cent of men and 10 per cent of women rated their health as poor, which suggests that some people with disabilities still rated their health as good. In care homes, 43 per cent of men aged 65–79 reported their health as good or very good, while, among those aged 80 and over, the proportion rose to more than one in two men (52 per cent). Among women, the differences by age were not marked: 52 per cent of those aged 65–79 and 54 per cent of those aged 80 and over perceived their health as good or very good. Again, this suggests that disability is not automatically reflected in perceptions of overall health.

The data shows wide variation between individual older people, with some suffering from many health problems, having substantial functional limitations and using services extensively, with others having few problems. Those using hospital health services (including outpatients and accident and emergency departments) were more likely to be living in private households and to have a long-standing illness or disability. People in care homes, however, tended to consult GPs more – perhaps because any longstanding illness they had was managed in the care home, and health crises were dealt with by GPs rather than by accident and emergency department visits.

Those people with few problems who did not use services fit some definitions of 'successful ageing' found in the literature, and which correspond to some of the aspects of heroic ageing models. One of the definitions of successful ageing commonly used in the literature is that developed by Rowe and Kahn (1997), which included three components: avoidance of disability, maintenance of physical functioning and active engagement with life. This bio-medical emphasis on physical functioning and activity is reflected in the use of the expression in popular literature and consumer information, and fits with notions of heroic ageing. Over time, it has undergone subtle changes in definition and scope, and has moved from a simple descriptive and technical term, to one that has become increasingly contested.

In its original bio-medical sense, 'successful ageing' is an expression that refers to the ability of organisms and species to live long enough to reproduce. This idea finds its most overt expression in the 'disposable soma' theory of ageing. This states that organisms, humans included, sacrifice some functions and incur some damage in order to ensure the continuance of the germ-line (i.e. the genetic material which will ensure the survival of the species). As such, ageing is seen as the loss of function inherent in growing older but from the perspective of species survival, not on an important scale. It would become important only if organisms did not survive long enough to pass on their genes to their offspring (Kirkwood, 1977).

This notion of successful ageing is limited in the way it helps us to understand the social, psychological and philosophical elements of growing older, simply describing the process from an evolutionary perspective. Other bio-medical theories of growing older, however, make links between biology, life style and environment, and look at successful ageing at an individual level. Theories of ageing, such as those based on models of accumulation of cell damage, for example, start to suggest ways in which this damage can be prevented or lessened. The suggestion that ageing can be prevented changes the idea of successful ageing from simply surviving until after reproduction, to maintaining function and avoiding disease. Fries (1980), for example, has proposed the notion of 'compressed morbidity' as an ideal – that people survive to a late age and only suffer health problems for a short period towards the end of life.

These ideas form the basis of much self-help literature and consumer material. One book entitled *Successful Aging* (Klein and Bloom, 1997) is written for professionals working with older people and older people themselves, and contains advice on diet, exercise and life style. The Positive Ageing website (www.healthandage.com) similarly contains information on diet and exercise including vitamin and herbal supplements, and complementary therapies. Research literature also takes the term 'successful ageing' to mean growing older without loss of function or health and, to this end, there are many evaluations of interventions, treatments and strategies for maintaining and promoting health.

The emphasis in the successful ageing literature is on physical functioning – something that can exclude those who, like some of our interviewees, are disabled. This idea of optimal physical functioning, however, has been connected to psychological functioning, in that there is also an emphasis on having a 'positive attitude' to growing older. This positive attitude consists of a refusal to accept the physical consequences of growing older as being inevitably life-limiting, or to see growing older as a process of decline which cannot be halted. While some of this literature encourages people to challenge their assumptions and stereotypes, there is also a potential negative consequence – that people feel guilty or inadequate if they are unable to overcome difficulties. Strawbridge (2000) has described the idea of 'successful ageing', which has developed particularly in America, as implying a kind of contest. However, as Strawbridge argues, 'people should never be told that they failed ageing because they had arthritis' (Strawbridge, 2000, p. 14).

The notion of 'successful ageing', therefore, offers some challenges to fatalistic ideas about growing older, but carries with it some limiting assumptions. One such limitation is that the idea of successful ageing as having minimum physical consequences does not consider other views which may be expressed by those who have physical problems, but who still regard themselves as healthy or enjoying their later years. The Bryant study, for example, discussed the concept of health as 'going and doing something meaningful' but pointed out that this did not necessarily mean physical activity, and some respondents had indicated that meaningful activity might involve only mental or cognitive processes.

This distinction between health and physical functioning or disease-free states may explain some studies which have found that older people tend to rate their health higher than would be expected if their physical condition was taken into account. Such findings indicate that, while physical health may be important in being able to go and do something meaningful, it is not the only factor.

Resources

The Bryant model also incorporates 'resources' and much of the literature accessed in this study related to the different resources that older people draw on. As with the Bryant model, there was much discussion and exploration of social support from family and friends as a resource, but, in other respects, the literature reflected other types of resource, namely income and monetary resources. This was also reflected in the focus groups, although an important point was made about money which emphasised the way in which it is valued, not as an end in itself, but as a means to an end. The discussion arose because of the use of the term 'comfortable healthy ageing' in the introduction to the focus group. Because of the association made by the group between 'comfortable' and being reasonably affluent, they queried the importance of money, arguing that it wasn't money that was important, but what it enabled you to do. Again, this reflects the Bryant model in which resources are elements that facilitate older people 'going and doing something meaningful'.

In talking about resources here, we have found it useful to use Arber and Ginn's notion of a triangle of resources – caring resources, material resources and health resources (Arber and Ginn, 1991; henceforth referred to as the 'Arber and Ginn model'). The health resources that Arber and Ginn discuss, however, are very similar to those identified by the Bryant model as 'abilities' with the main difference being the discussion of health-care services as resources. To avoid duplication, we have chosen to discuss health, function and service use under the heading of 'abilities' to maintain congruence with the Bryant model, and the discussion of resources will cover only caring resources and material resources.

Caring resources

Caring resources, according to the Arber and Ginn model, include the support of friends and family, and this is reflected in much of the work that has looked at older people and their social networks. This caring may go on in addition to, or instead of, services provided by health and social care agencies, and, because of its informal nature, it has proved difficult to explore. There are, however, some studies which have explored informal support, and which indicate the value that this has for the perceived and actual health and functioning of older people.

There is a connection between physical health and social engagement made in some literature, and some of the discussions in our focus groups and interviews suggested that this is a key measure of health for some older people. The ability to make and maintain relationships with friends and family is an important part of social roles, and the ability to fulfil these roles is a key to feeling healthy. This is not the same as engaging in physical activities, but physical abilities do enter into it. The ability to get around to meet people, the ability to be a good host if they come to visit you (providing food and drinks, for example), and the ability to communicate clearly all depend on physical abilities to some extent. In this sense, physical abilities become, not ends in themselves, but means to an end. The focus of enjoyment therefore becomes the social interaction and the relationships involved.

Conversely, social support, that is the help and assistance offered by social networks and agencies, has been found by some studies to lead to a decrease in functional ability. The message seems to be that, while active social engagement is beneficial for health, social support can undermine function and independence. It is therefore not just social interaction *per se* that is good for health, but the type of interaction involved. Emotional support rather than instrumental support has been found to be associated with better physical functioning (Pennix *et al.*, 1997), and Berkman has suggested that this is because emotional support involves the important quality of intimacy (Berkman, 1995).

Research into the types of interaction that older people have has focused variously on the type of interaction, the quality, the intensity or frequency and the characteristics of the participants. Antonucci (1989) has examined interaction with families, finding that family members make up more than half of support networks. The extent to which family contact increases satisfaction or quality of life, however, is less clear. While family members may provide support and care, it is not necessarily the case that this involves enhanced quality of life. A sense of obligation rather than intimacy may drive family support and it may exclude reciprocity in the relationship, a feature of many friendships (Jackson and Antonucci, 1987). Many studies have indicated that the support of friends is more important to self-perceived well-being than the support of families (Larson *et al.*, 1986; O'Connor, 1995).

There is also some evidence that the friendships that older people have tend to be very stable and enduring (Field and Minkler, 1988). While friendships may wax and wane with time (Carstenson, 1991), older people's perceptions of support remain stable. Bosse *et al.* (1990) and Dean *et al.* (1992) have suggested that this may be due to a process of selectivity, as older people focus more on long-term friendships and less on developing new ones. Conversely, a longitudinal study by Jerrome and Wenger (1999) has shown that older people can and do replace friends who move away, become ill or die, and that networks change as people age and their circumstances change.

Siebert *et al.* (1999) have suggested that one way of understanding the dynamics of social support is to examine its effects on the role identity of the older person. They describe role identity as 'the character and role we devise for ourselves as an occupant of a particular social position' (Siebert *et al.*, 1999, p. 524). The relationships that we have with others can either support or disrupt our role identities, which is important in maintaining the roles to which we are strongly committed. Siebert *et al.* suggest that increased support from family members, therefore, 'threatens older adults' self-perception as competent, giving people while bolstering their role identities as needy dependents' (Siebert *et al.*, 1999, p. 529). Role theory offers an explanation of the apparently contradictory findings of much of the social engagement research. It is not the quantity of social contact that is important, therefore, but its effects on how we see ourselves.

Personal outlooks

The third element of the Bryant model is 'attitude'. This term can have a range of meanings, from the colloquial sense of 'approach to life', to the precise use in psychology, where it would be used in reference to specific phenomena (such as attitudes to political movements or hospital treatment). In view of this potential confusion, we have used the term 'personal outlooks' to indicate general approaches or views in a range of areas. The Bryant model in part reflects this breadth, as it discusses the attitudes of older people to ill health and growing older. The following discussion is correspondingly inclusive rather than narrow.

Self-efficacy

One concept in the academic literature on personal outlooks is the concept of 'self-efficacy'. Bandura (1986) proposed the concept of 'self-efficacy' as a development of social cognitive theory, which suggests that human activity is shaped by forethought and belief. Self-efficacy is the belief in one's ability to do something, Bandura argues, and this is an important determinant in deciding to do it. Low self-efficacy, therefore, would result in people making less effort or persevering for less time with some activities or avoiding them altogether.

Some of the evaluation studies of exercise have used as a baseline assessment a measure of self-efficacy. In such studies, participants are asked to rate their strength of expectation that they could complete certain tasks using a scale that ranges from high uncertainty to complete certitude. Self-efficacy was used to predict participation in exercise programmes by Resnick *et al.* (2000), for example. This study suggested that there were several different pathways or influences on self-efficacy, including physical health, mental health, age and gender. These factors influenced exercise outcome expectations and therefore self-efficacy. The higher someone's feelings of self-efficacy, the more likely they were to be active, and some studies have shown that this is not closely related to the severity of a health problem or functional difficulty (Seeman *et al.*, 1999). Some scales measure activity on a wide range of activities, such as shopping and leisure, while others focus on small-scale behaviours, such as walking and housework. The assumption behind the use of all these scales, however, is that there are connections between self-efficacy and willingness to participate in activities, both physical and social.

While self-efficacy has been defined mainly as being about physical confidence, the literature suggests that it can have implications for social activities as well. Seeing yourself as able and well is related to how you think others see you, and therefore whether you feel confident in getting to know new people, or maintaining old relationships. Going to a social event and feeling confident that you will be able to join in activities without mishap or difficulty is a key factor in making a decision to go. Low self-efficacy may prevent people from even trying activities. If the expectation is that it will end in disaster, then the risks to self-esteem and public persona are too high. The study conducted by

Seeman *et al.* suggests that low expectations about interpersonal relationships (i.e. that they will not be successful) are not related to functional abilities (Seeman *et al.*, 1999). This conclusion suggests that self-efficacy belief might best be thought of as specific rather than general and that more differentiation is needed if the effects of self-efficacy are to be more fully understood.

Self-efficacy is clearly an important factor in deciding to engage in activities and the benefits of engagement seem to be an increased satisfaction with life. It is therefore surprising that there seems to be little work looking at ways of increasing self-efficacy or confidence in older people. While self-efficacy is considered as a predictor of participation, and is sometimes included as an outcome measure in studies, there seems to be little work that concentrates on developing self-efficacy, and so it is unclear how it could be fostered and also what might lower or damage it.

Quality of life

Another area of the literature deals with the broad question of how older people define the quality of life and what is important to them. As a concept, quality of life comes close to the ideas of comfortable healthy ageing, in that it deals not just with how older people judge their quality of life, but also with what they think contributes to this. As Farquhar (1995) has pointed out, the term 'quality of life' has become popular, even clichéd. She traces its use back to the end of the Second World War when people became more concerned with reaching beyond the basics to sustain life, and aspired to better goods and services. This materialistic emphasis, however, has not been demonstrated by studies that have asked older people what they feel contributes to their quality of life. An Age Concern study in 1974, for example, found that health and the ability to engage in activities and relationships was most important in this respect.

As Farquhar argues, quality of life has been problematic in the health-care field, mainly because professionals have 'a limited perception of the concept' (Farquhar, 1995, p. 1440). Broadening out the concept of quality of life beyond objective measures, such as health and functional status or socio-economic status, may mean moving into an exploration of subjective dimensions such as self-esteem and satisfaction with life. As several researchers have pointed out, however, such an approach does not guarantee that measures will reflect the views of older people rather than researchers (Haas, 1999; O'Boyle et al., 1998).

Those studies that have asked older people to specify their view of quality of life have found that it can differ from the expectations of younger people. Farquhar (1995) also found that the determinants of quality of life differed between semi-rural and inner-city areas. For example, those living in poorer material and environmental circumstances would identify these elements as important, while people who enjoyed better circumstances would not mention these aspects. Aspects of living that are not immediately problematic may be taken for granted and not identified as important determinants of life quality.

Amidst all of this individual variation, O'Boyle et al. (1998) has developed a tool that allows individual elements of life quality for older people to be identified and weighted in an overall scoring process. Not surprisingly, there are some core elements but the tool allows for considerable variation between individuals.

Other studies have looked at the relationship between quality of life scores and factors such as health, psychological and social factors. Good health, social participation and a sense of purpose have been found to be related to higher ratings of quality of life – more so than material or financial circumstances (Bowling et al., 2002). In constructing a model through multiple regression analysis, the study by Bowling et al. (2002) found that social comparisons and expectations were important in determining self-rated quality of life, as were personality and social capital (support networks and social relationships). In other words, older people rated their quality of life in relation to their expectations and counted social interactions as important (the resources in the Bryant model). Other authors have argued that there is some link between personality and quality of life ratings. For example, Hagberg et al. (2002) found that emotional stability was related to psychological well-being and, interestingly, original thinking was related to increased psychosomatic symptoms.

Studies have looked at perceptions of quality of life among older people in different settings, including their own homes and in long-term care. Few studies have compared older people in different settings. Studies usually focus on one group at a time, depending on the resources they have to involve and include different groups in the research. There is not much indication that factors that determine quality of life are very different in different groups. Bearing in mind that the General Household Survey 1998 (2000) indicated that people in care homes had higher levels of disability than those in private residences, this suggests that physical health may not be as important to quality of life as might be assumed. Guse and Masesar (1999), for example, found that relationships with others were important to people in long-term care – a finding that echoes the results of research with other older people living in their own homes. What Guse and Masesar also found, however, was that 'being helpful to others' was also valued – a finding that challenges notions of people in care homes as receivers rather than givers of help.

Overall, the literature indicates that relationships are strong determinants of quality of life. In other words, if people feel engaged in social relationships, this will lead to them evaluating their quality of life more highly. The importance of relationships and the ability to engage in them may be mediated by individual characteristics, backgrounds and skills, but it would appear to be a consistent feature of much quality of life research.

Sense of coherence

One concept that was found in the process of searching the literature, although it was not searched for explicitly, is that of 'sense of coherence'. This was defined by Antonovsky (1979, p. 13) as 'the confidence that the world is structured, predictable and explicable, that you have the resources to meet the demands of the environment, and that these demands are worth responding to.' The concept therefore has three elements – comprehensibility, manageability and meaningfulness of the world. One problem with the 'sense of coherence' concept, however, is that, like many other ideas, while it is applied to older people, it is not developed from them. As such, it has little evidence supporting its relevance to older people, and may simply be a construct derived from younger people's views of what is desirable. Again, the concept of 'successful ageing' rears its head, this time linked to a 'sense of coherence' as the goal to strive for.

Having something meaningful to do

The fourth, and perhaps most important part, of the Bryant model is having something meaningful to do. This can be a variety of things, and some of these, such as relationships with family and friends, have already been mentioned. Each individual may have different definitions of what is meaningful to them, perhaps an activity that represents continuity with past activities (lifelong hobbies for example) or perhaps new activities that may have been an ambition in the past or that may indeed be an unexpected discovery.

Following from the Bryant model, the literature on relationships as something meaningful (rather than as a resource, as discussed above) was surveyed. There is a body of literature that suggests that engagement in social activities and relationships is associated with a slower decline in functional status (Unger *et al.*, 1997). Similarly, activities such as housework and shopping have been associated with better health and function by several researchers, including Glass *et al.* (1995) and Horgas *et al.* (1998). In these studies, however, it is difficult to disentangle cause and effect. Do people do more housework because they feel more able, or does doing housework make you feel better? Similarly, leisure activities, such as attending education classes, have also been associated with better functioning (Berkman, 1995). However, as the discussion on self-efficacy suggests, this may be because higher levels of confidence lead to more participation. Interestingly, leisure activities which are not exercise-based, and which may be quite sedentary, have been identified as an important part of older people's activities by Horgas *et al.* (1998) who suggested that having a range of activities was important.

Gerotranscendence and sageing

One interesting concept in the literature is 'gerotranscendence', which attempts to pull all of this diverse and somewhat contradictory material together, and offers some definitions of healthy ageing that are independent of physical functioning. Tornstam (1996) has described this as a shift from the material and rational concerns of younger adulthood towards a perspective on life which transcends these elements, and which focuses more on the spiritual and meditative. This concept offers a way of thinking about growing older that challenges materialistic goals that may be of more salience to younger people. However, it does have some negative connotations and potential interpretations. In particular, the move away from materialism could be interpreted as a reason for failing to pay much attention to the material circumstances of older people.

Some studies have been carried out which have looked at the idea of gerotranscendence in more depth. They have found, variously, that older people show some tendencies to become less materialistic, less preoccupied with deadlines and time limits, and less concerned about their public image. Correspondingly, they become more comfortable with their life situation and the relationships that they have. Gerotranscendence offers a different approach to thinking about growing older, which avoids the problems of imposing goals and values that are about defeating age, but runs some other risks. It is not clear how gerotranscendence can be distinguished from other models of ageing, such as disengagement theory, which argues that a 'normal' part of growing older is to become less interested in and engaged with everyday living. Indeed, Tornstam did make the links between the two theories, arguing that disengagement theory had been unjustly abandoned (Jonson and Magnussen, 2001). The problem with disengagement theory is that it can be used as a rationale for assuming that older people do not want to be active and engaged and, by default, denying them opportunities and support to do so.

'Sageing' (de Rozario, 1998) is an idea which draws from a range of different cultural traditions to suggest ways in which older people may grow and develop across the life course, and in some cultures be increasingly respected for their wisdom and life experience. Torres (1999), for example, has argued that many of our ideas about successful ageing are based on the values of western industrial society, and this blinds us to other ways of thinking in other cultures. The Sufi notion of spiritual growth over the life course, for example, is of a process whereby identification with others becomes stronger and sense of self as a separate entity becomes weaker (Lewin, 2000). This stands in sharp contrast to western notions of individualism. Similarly, Torres

(1999) has pointed to differences in the value placed on independence in older age, demonstrated in the West, and the value placed on being loved enough to be cared for in Hong Kong.

In western cultures, alternatives to materialistic and physical models of ageing are suggested by studies of older people and their spirituality and worship practices. Some of this literature fails to disentangle spirituality from church-going or membership of a religious group from the general life style that is associated with membership. Armer and Conn (2001) have gone some way towards clarifying these factors by referring to public or formal involvement, private or informal involvement and subjective self-reports of religious life style. In their review of the literature, they have suggested that 'formal religiosity' has been linked to reduced hospital stays and to increased life-satisfaction. They cite some researchers as suggesting that, because of the low cost and availability of religious activity, the relationship between this and health-care costs should be investigated. While investigations of the relationship between religiosity and other variables, such as physical health, depression and mortality, may be made, there is little which explores religiosity *per se*. Religion is largely studied as a means to an end (usually increased physical health), and not as a potential source of new ideas and models of healthy ageing.

5 CONCLUSIONS

This review has covered an extensive and diverse range of literature. The process of locating it and retrieving it was complex, as was the process of analysing it once we had got it. This complexity was largely due to the fact that the brief, which had made sense to us and to the commissioning group, had not matched up with the search terms and keywords found in the academic literature. This points to the overall conclusion that can be drawn from the study, which is that the academic and funding body models and ways of thinking about growing older reflect their concerns and views rather than those of older people.

These differences are particularly striking when looking at what has been written about ageing and health. The focus of the material reflects the discipline and history of the researchers, in the way that they define concepts, make links between them and carry out studies. This is particularly the case with very structured research, which seeks to measure phenomena. Such research has to predefine concepts, and operationalise them in terms of scales and measures, and so leaves little room for the voices of older people to be heard in an unstructured way.

Across this literature, two models of growing older can be discerned – the heroic model and the deficit model. The heroic model sees ageing as an enemy to be fought, and regards submission to the effects of time as a defeat and a failure. It can be seen in many of the discussions on successful ageing, but also in many of the other areas, where efforts are made to identify strategies for defeating or postponing ageing. It is also evident in media stories about active elders and adverts for miracle anti-ageing drugs and creams. The converse of this is the deficit model, where decline is seen as inevitable and efforts are made to identify ways of coping with increasing impairment. While this model may not set unrealistic goals, its pessimistic assumptions crowd out useful debate about goals and values which are independent of physical functioning.

In other words, the literature does not seem to give any room to inclusive definitions of health for all older people, including those with some sort of physical problem and those who are well. In the heroic model, problems are seen as failures and, in the deficit model, they are seen as an inevitable consequence of growing older. While the heroic model celebrates wellness, it runs the risk of excluding those who are not well. What are not discussed to any great extent are the models that older people themselves may have.

The few studies that did ask older people about their definitions of health indicated ways of thinking that moved beyond simple physical functioning. Older people valued meaningful activity and adapted their goals to their circumstances. There are further questions that can be asked about meaningful activity for older people. For example, what makes an activity meaningful? How does the meaning of an activity change over the life course? What are the values that underpin meaning? We also need to develop systems and processes for finding out about older people's meanings and responding to differences among these.

There are further research questions that follow on from this, and these are about the resources that older people may need to help them to 'go and do something meaningful'. These may be material resources, such as money, transport, facilities, or they may be social and psychological, such as support, information and advice.

We also need to think about the personal outlooks of older people, their expectations, values and attitudes, as these shape models of health. We should be cautious about attributing all health beliefs and behaviours to attitudes, and we should be especially vigilant to guard against ideas that there are right and wrong attitudes that older people can have. Nonetheless, the work on personal outlooks does point to differences among older people, and also to the possibilities for change and development. Incorporating these ideas into planning and delivering support seems to be essential, but, for this to happen, we need to know more about the differences between individuals and the impact these differences have on their models of health.

To return to the title of this report, *Getting Old is not for Cowards*, we need to be finding ways of making bravery less essential for what is a normal and natural part of life. We need to find ways of supporting people to be healthy as they grow older in effective and efficient ways. To do this, however, we need to find out more about their ideas and models of health, and rely less on the models found in research and the media.

Bibliography

References (literature cited in the text of the report)

Age Concern (1974) *Older People in the United Kingdom: Some Basic Facts*. London: Age Concern

Antonovsky, A. (1979) *Health, Stress and Coping: New Perspectives on Mental and Physical Well-being*. San Francisco, CA: Jossey-Bass

Antonucci, T.C. (1989) 'Understanding adult social relationships', in K. Kreppner and R.M. Lerner (eds) *Family Systems and Life-span Development*. Hillside, NJ: Lawrence Erlbaum, pp. 303–17

Arber, S. and Ginn, J. (1991) *Gender and Later Life: A Sociological Analysis of Resources and Constraints*. London: Sage

Armer, J.M. and Conn, V.S. (2001) 'Exploration of spirituality and health among diverse rural elderly individuals', *Journal of Gerontological Nursing*, Vol. 27, No. 6, pp. 28–37

Bandura, A. (1986) *Social Foundations of Thought and Action: A Social Cognitive Theory*. Englewood Cliffs, NJ: Prentice-Hall

Berkman, L.F. (1995) 'The role of social relations in health promotion', *Psychosomatic Medicine*, Vol. 57, No. 3, pp. 245–54

Bosse, R., Aldwin, C.M., Levenson, M.R., Workman-Daniels, K. and Ekerdt, D.J. (1990) 'Differences in social support among retirees and workers: findings from the normative aging study', *Psychology and Aging*, Vol. 5, No. 1, pp. 41–7

Bowling, A., Banister, D., Sutton, S., Evans, O. and Windsor, J. (2002) 'A multidimensional model of the quality of life in older age', *Aging and Mental Health*, Vol. 6, No. 4, pp. 355–71

Bryant, L.L., Corbett, K.K. and Kutner, J.S. (2001) 'In their own words: a model of healthy aging', *Social Science and Medicine*, Vol. 53, No. 7, pp. 927–41

Carstenson, L.L. (1991) 'Selectivity theory: social activity in life-span context', in K.W. Schaie (ed.) *Annual Review of Geroiatrics and Gerontology 11*. New York: Springer, pp. 195–217

Collins English Dictionary (1999) 4th edn. Glasgow: HarperCollins Publishers

Dean, A., Matt, G.E. and Wood, P. (1992) 'The effects of widowhood on social support from significant others', *Journal of Community Psychology*, Vol. 20, No. 4, pp. 309–25

de Rozario, L. (1998) 'From ageing to sageing: eldering and the art of being as occupation', *Journal of Occupational Science* (Australia), Vol. 5, No. 3, pp. 119–26

Farquhar, M. (1995) 'Elderly people's definitions of quality of life', *Social Science and Medicine*, Vol. 41, No. 10, pp. 1439–46

Field, D. and Minkler, M. (1988) 'Continuity and change in social support between young-old and old-old or very-old age', *Journal of Applied Gerontology*, Vol. 43, pp. 100–6

Fries, J.F. (1980) 'Ageing, natural death and the compression of morbidity', *New England Journal of Medicine*, Vol. 303, No. 3, pp. 130–6

General Household Survey 1998 (2000). London: The Stationery Office

Glass, T.A., Seeman, T.E., Herzog, A.R., Kahn, R. and Berkmann, L.F. (1995) 'Change in productive activity in late adulthood: MacArthur studies of successful ageing', *Journal of Gerontology; Social Sciences*, Vol. 50B, pp. S65–76

Guse, L.W. and Masesar, M.A. (1999) 'Quality of life and successful aging in long-term care: perceptions of residents', *Issues in Mental Health Nursing*, Vol. 20, No. 6, pp. 527–39

Haas, B. (1999) 'A multidisciplinary concept analysis of quality of life', *Western Journal of Nursing Research*, Vol. 21, No. 6, pp. 728–42

Hagberg, M., Hagberg, B. and Saveman, B.-I. (2002) 'The significance of personality factors for various dimensions of life quality among older people', *Aging and Mental Health*, Vol. 6, No. 2, pp. 178–185

Health Survey for England 2000 (2002) *The Health of Older People*. London: Stationery Office in conjunction with National Centre for Social Research, Department of Epidemiology and Public Health, University College London

Heathcote, G. (2000) 'Autonomy, health and ageing: transnational perspectives', *Health Education Research*, Vol. 15, No. 1, pp. 13–24

Horgas, A.L., Wilms, H. and Baltes, M.M. (1998) 'Daily life in very old age: everyday activities as expression of successful living', *The Gerontologist*, Vol. 38, pp. 556–68

Jackson, J.S. and Antonucci, T.C. (1987) 'Social network characteristics and psychological well-being: a replication and extension', *Health Education Quarterly*, Vol. 14, pp. 461–81

Jerrome, D. (1992) *Good Company: An Anthropological Study of Old People in Groups*. Edinburgh: Edinburgh University Press

Jerrome, D. and Wenger, G.C. (1999) 'Stability and change in late-life friendships', *Ageing and Society*, Vol. 19, No. 6, pp. 661–76

Jonson, H. and Magnussen, J.A. (2001) 'A new age of old age? Gerotranscendence and the re-enchantment of aging', *Journal of Aging Studies*, Vol. 15, No. 4, pp. 317–31

Kirkwood, T.B.L. (1977) 'Evolution of ageing', *Nature*, Vol. 270, pp. 301–4

Klein, W.C. and Bloom, M. (1997) *Successful Aging: Strategies for Healthy Living*. New York: Plenum Press

Larson, R., Mannell, R. and Zuzanek, J. (1986) 'Daily well-being of older adults with friends and family', *Psychology and Aging*, Vol. 1, pp. 117–26

Lewin, F.A. (2000) 'Development towards wisdom and maturity: Sufi conception of self', *Journal of Ageing and Identity*, Vol. 5, No. 3, pp. 137–49

NHS CRD (Centre for Reviews and Dissemination) (2001) *Undertaking Systematic Reviews of Research on Effectiveness. CRD's Guidance for those Carrying out or Commissioning Reviews*. CRD Report No. 4, 2nd edn. York: CRD. http://www.york.ac.uk/inst/crd/report4.htm (accessed 10 February 2003)

O'Boyle, C.A., McGee, H.M. and Joyce, C.R.B. (1998) *Individual Quality of Life: Approaches to Conceptualisation and Measurement in Health*. Reading, MA: Hardwood Academic

O'Connor, B.P. (1995) 'Family and friend relationships among older and younger adults: interaction motivation, mood and quality', *International Journal of Aging and Human Development*, Vol. 40, No. 1, pp. 9–29

Pennix, B.W., van Tilburg, T., Kriegsman, D.M.W., Deeg, D.J.H., Boeke, A.J.P. and van Eijk, J.T.M. (1997) 'Effects of social support and personal coping resources on mortality on older age: the longitudinal aging study, Amsterdam', *American Journal of Epidemiology*, Vol. 146, pp. 510–19

Resnick, B., Palmer, M.H., Jenkins, L.S. and Spellbring, A.M. (2000) 'Path analysis of efficacy expectations and exercise behaviour in older adults', *Journal of Advanced Nursing*, Vol. 31, No. 6, pp. 1309–15

Rowe, J.W. and Kahn, R.L. (1997) 'Successful ageing', *The Gerontologist*, Vol. 37, No. 2, pp. 433–40

Seeman, T.E., Unger, J.B., McAvay, G. and Mendes de Leon, C.F. (1999) 'Self-efficacy beliefs and perceived declines in functional ability: MacArthur studies of successful ageing', *Journals of Gerontology, Series B, Psychological Sciences and Social Sciences*, Vol. 54B, No. 4, pp. P214–22

Siebert, D.C., Mutran, E.J. and Reitzes, D.C. (1999) 'Friendship and social support: the importance of role identity to ageing', *Social Work*, Vol. 44, No. 6, pp. 522–33

Strawbridge, W. (2000) 'Chronic illness: coping successfully for successful ageing', *Aging Today*, September/October, pp. 14–15

Tornstam, L. (1996) 'Gerotranscendence – a theory about maturing in old age', *Journal of Ageing and Identity*, Vol. 1, No. 1, pp. 37–50

Torres, S. (1999) 'A culturally relevant theoretical framework for the study of successful ageing', *Ageing and Society*, Vol. 19, No. 1, pp. 35–51

Unger, J.B., Johnson, C.A. and Marks, G. (1997) 'Functional decline in the elderly: evidence for direct and stress-buffering protective effects of social interactions and physical activity', *Annals of Behavioural Medicine*, Vol. 19, pp. 152–60

Further reading (literature which provided contextual background to the project but which is not cited in the text of the report)

Aging Today (2000) 'Chronic illness: coping successfully for successful aging', *Aging Today*, Vol. 21, No. 5, p. 14

Arber, S. and Cooper, H. (1999) 'Gender differences in health in later life', *Social Science and Medicine*, Vol. 48, No. 1, pp. 61–76

Bauman, A.E. and Smith, B.J. (2000) 'Healthy ageing: what role can physical activity play?', *Medical Journal of Australia*, Vol. 173, No. 2, pp. 88–90

Bergstrom, M.J. and Holmes, M.E. (2000) 'Lay theories of successful aging after the death of a spouse: a network text analysis of bereavement advice', *Health Communication*, Vol. 12, No. 4, pp. 377–406

Brunell, M. (2001) 'Doing for others: it gives me something to do. An ethnographic study of older, urban women living alone in poverty', Columbia University Teachers' College, Ed.D

Burbank, P.M. (1988) 'Meaning in life among older persons', Boston University, DNSC

Carlson, M., Clark, F. and Young, B. (1987) 'Practical contributions of occupational science to the art of successful ageing: how to sculpt a meaningful life in older adulthood', *Journal of Occupational Science* (Australia), Vol. 5, No. 3, pp. 107–18

Connor, M. (2000) 'Recreational folk dance: a multicultural exercise component in healthy ageing', *Australian Occupational Therapy Journal*, Vol. 47, No. 2, pp. 69–76

Delaney, N.E. (1991) 'Direct and indirect effects of variables related to locus-of-control on life satisfaction as reported by community-dwelling and nursing home older adults', the University of Toledo, PhD

Dello Buono, M., Uriuoli, O. and De Leo, D. (1998) 'Quality of life and longevity: study of centenarians', *Age and Ageing*, Vol. 27, No. 2, pp. 207–16

Everard, K.M., Lach, H.W., Fisher, E.B. and Baum, M.C. (2000) 'Relationship of activity and social support to the functional health of older adults', *Journals of Gerontology, Series B, Psychological Sciences and Social Sciences*; Vol. 55B, No. 4, pp. S208–12

Fielf, E.M., Walker, M.H. and Orrell, M.W. (2002) 'Social networks and health of older people living in sheltered housing', *Aging and Mental Health*, Vol. 6, No. 4, pp. 372–86

Ford, A.B., Haug, M.R., Stange, K.C., Gaines, A.D., Noekler, L.S. and Jones, P.K. (2000) 'Sustained personal autonomy: a measure of successful aging', *Journal of Aging and Health*, Vol. 12, No. 4, pp. 470–89

Gama, E.V., Damian, J.E., Perez de Molino, J., Lopez, M.R, Lopez Perez, M. and Gavira Iglesias, F.J. (2000) 'Association of individual activities of daily living with self-rated health in older people', *Age and Ageing*, Vol. 29, No. 3, pp. 267–70

Godfrey, M. (2001) 'Prevention: developing a framework for conceptualizing and evaluating outcomes of preventive services for older people', *Health and Social Care in the Community*, Vol. 9, No. 2, pp. 89–99

Gow, J., Webster, N., Gilhooly, M., Hamilton, K., O'Neill, M., Edgerton. E. and Pike, F. (2001) 'Transport, aging and quality of life: findings from qualitative aspects of a comparative study', *The Gerontologist*, Vol. 41, No. 1, p. 231

Hays, J.C., Saunders, W.B., Flint, E.P., Kaplan, B.H. and Blazer, D.G. (1997) 'Social support and depression as risk factors for loss of physical function in late life', *Aging and Mental Health*, Vol. 1, No. 3, pp. 209–20

Help the Aged (2002) *Active Ageing. Help the Aged Policy Statement July 2002*. London: Help the Aged

Hugman, R. (1999) 'Ageing, occupation and social engagement: towards a lively later life', *Journal of Occupational Science* (Australia), Vol. 6, No. 2, pp. 61–7

Johnson, P.W. (1981) 'The correlates of psychological well-being of urban elderly residents of public housing. 1981', EBM Reviews – Cochrane Controlled Trials Register. Accession No. CN-00241212 (no additional source data available)

Kalache, A. and Kickbusch, I. (1997) 'A global strategy for healthy ageing', *World Health*, Vol. 4, pp. 4–5

Keasberry, I.N. (2001) 'Elder care and intergenerational relationships in rural Yogyakarta, Indonesia', *Ageing and Society*, Vol. 21, No. 5, pp. 641–65

Kendig, H., Koyano, W., Asakawa, T. and Takatoshi, A. (1999) 'Social support of older people in Australia and Japan', *Ageing and Society*, Vol. 19, No. 2, pp. 185–207

Kubzansky, L.D., Berkman, L.F. and Seeman, T.E. (2000) 'Social conditions and distress in elderly persons: findings from the MacArthur studies of successful ageing, *Journals of Gerontology, Series B, Psychological Sciences and Social Sciences*, Vol. 55B, No. 4, pp. P238–46

Lewis, J.S. (1996) 'Sense of coherence and the strengths perspective with older persons', *Journal of Gerontological Social Work*, Vol. 26, Nos 3/4, pp. 99–112

Lundh, U. and Nolan, M. (1996a) 'Ageing and quality of life 1: towards a better understanding', *British Journal of Nursing*, Vol. 5, No. 20, pp. 1248–51

Lundh, U. and Nolan, M. (1996b) 'Ageing and quality of life 2: understanding successful ageing', *British Journal of Nursing*, Vol. 5, No. 21, pp. 1291–5

Mackenzie, E.R., Rajagopal, D.E., Meibohm, M. and Lavizzo-Mourey, R. (2000) 'Spiritual support and psychological well-being: older adults' perceptions of the religion and health connection', *Alternative Therapies in Health and Medicine*, Vol. 6, No. 6, pp. 37–45

Magnani, L.E. (1990) 'Hardiness, self-perceived health, and activity among independently functioning older adults ... including commentary by Hadley, B.J.', *Scholarly Inquiry for Nursing Practice*, Vol. 4, No. 3, pp. 171–88

Marinelli, R.D. and Plummer, O.K. (1999) 'Healthy aging: beyond exercise. Activities', *Adaptation and Aging*, Vol. 23, No. 4, pp. 1–11

Martin, M., Grünendahl, M. and Martin, P. (2001) 'Age difference in stress, social resources, and well-being in middle and older age', *Journals of Gerontology, Series B, Psychological Sciences and Social Sciences*, Vol. 56B, No. 4, pp. P214–22

Michael, Y.L., Colditz, G.A., Coakley, E. and Kawachi, I. (1999) 'Health behaviors, social networks, and healthy aging: cross-sectional evidence from the Nurses' Health Study', *Quality of Life Research*, Vol. 8, No. 8, pp. 711–22

Miller, M.P. (1991) 'Factors promoting wellness in the aged person: an ethnographic study', *Advances in Nursing Science*, Vol. 13, No. 4, pp. 38–51

Miller, S.M. (1997) 'Successful aging in America – Part 6: antioxidants and aging', *Medical Laboratory Observer*, Vol. 29, No. 9, pp. 42–3, 46–53

Mor-Barak, M.E. and Tynan, M. (1993) 'Older workers and the workplace: a new challenge for occupational social work', *Social Work*, Vol. 38, No. 1, pp. 45–55

Moore, S.L., Metcalf, B. and Schow, E. (2000) 'Aging and meaning in life: examining the concept', *Geriatric Nursing*, Vol. 21, No. 1, pp. 27–9

Morgan, K., Dallosso, H., Bassey, E.J., Ebrahim, S., Fentem, P.H. and Arie, T.H. (1991) 'Customary physical activity, psychological well-being and successful ageing', *Ageing and Society*, Vol. 11, No. 4, pp. 399–415

Mull, C.S. (1989) 'Interrelationships of religiosity, social resources, coping responses, health, and well-being among older adults', University of Illinois at Chicago, Health Sciences Center, PhD

Nelson, H.C. (1997) 'To move or not to move: the role of health and well-being', *Health Care in Later Life*, Vol. 2, No. 3, pp. 143–54

Nilsson, M., Ekmann, S.L., Ericsson, K. and Winblad, B. (1996) 'Some characteristics of the quality of life in old age illustrated by means of Allardt's concept', *Scandinavian Journal of Caring Sciences*, Vol. 10, No. 2, pp. 116–21

Nilsson, M., Ekman, S. and Sarvimaki, A. (1998) 'Ageing with joy or resigning to old age: older people's experiences of the quality of life in old age', *Health Care in Later Life*, Vol. 3, No. 2, pp. 94–110

Nocon, A. and Pearson, M. (2000) 'The roles of friends and neighbours in providing support for older people', *Ageing and Society*, Vol. 20, No. 3, pp. 341–67

Nolan, M. (2001) 'Successful ageing: keeping the "person" in person-centred care', *British Journal of Nursing*, Vol. 10, No. 7, pp. 450–4

Pangman, V.C. and Seguire, M. (2000) 'Sexuality and the chronically ill older adult: a social justice issue', *Sexuality and Disability*, Vol. 18, No. 1, pp. 49–59

Parker, M.W., Fuller, G.F., Koenig, H.G., Bellis, J.M., Vaitkus, M.A., Barko, W.F. and Eitzen, J. (2001) 'Soldier and family wellness across the life course: a developmental model of successful aging, spirituality, and health promotion, Part II', *Military Medicine*, Vol. 166, No. 7, pp. 561–70

Partridge, C., Johnston, M. and Morris, L. (1996) 'Disability and health: perceptions of a sample of elderly people', *Physiotherapy Research International*, Vol. 1, No. 1, pp. 17–29

Perrig-Chiello, P., Perrig, W.J. and Stähelin, H.B. (1999) 'Health control beliefs in old age – relationship with subjective and objective health, and health behaviour', *Psychology Health and Medicine*, Vol. 4, No. 1, pp. 83–94

Phillipson, C., Bernard, M., Phillips, J. and Ogg, J. (1998) 'The family and community life of older people: household composition and social networks in three urban areas', *Ageing and Society*, Vol. 18, No. 3, pp. 259–89

Pina, D.L. and Bengtson, V.L. (1995) 'Division of household labor and the well-being of retirement-aged wives', *The Gerontologist*, Vol. 35, No. 3, pp. 308–17

Prestoy, S.F. (1993) 'Quality of life as perceived and experienced through activity, relationships and sense of independence: an ethnography of seven urban older adults who attend a senior citizen's center', New York University, PhD

Rennemark, M. and Hagberg, B. (1997) 'Social network patterns among the elderly in relation to their perceived life history in an Eriksonian perspective', *Aging and Mental Health*, Vol. 1, No. 4, pp. 321–31

Rennemark, M and Hagberg, B. (1999) 'Gender specific associations between social network and health behaviour in old age', *Aging and Mental Health*, Vol. 3, No. 4, pp. 320–7

Roelofs, L.H. (1999) 'The meaning of leisure', *Journal of Gerontological Nursing*, Vol. 25, No. 10, pp. 32–9

Rosenkoetter, M.M. and Garris, J.M. (1998) 'Psychosocial changes following retirement', *Journal of Advanced Nursing*, Vol. 27, No. 5, pp. 966–76

Russell, C. and Schofield, T. (1999) 'Social isolation in old age: a qualitative exploration of service providers' perceptions, *Ageing and Society*, Vol. 19, No. 1, pp. 69–91

Schmitt, M. and Jüchtern, J. (2001) 'The structure of subjective well-being in middle adulthood', *Aging and Mental Health*, Vol. 5, No. 1, pp. 47–55

Seeman, T.E., Albert, M., Lusignolo, T.M. and Berkman, L. (2001) 'Social relationships, social support, and patterns of cognitive aging in healthy, high-functioning older adults: MacArthur studies of successful aging', *Health Psychology*, Vol. 20, No. 4, pp. 243–55

Seeman, T.E., Bruce, M.L. and McAvay, G.J. (1996) 'Social network characteristics and onset of ADL disability: MacArthur studies of successful aging', *Journals of Gerontology, Series B, Psychological Sciences and Social Sciences*, Vol. 51B, No. 4, pp. S191–200

Silver, R. (1999) 'Differences among aging and young adults in attitudes and cognition', *Art Therapy*, Vol. 16, No. 3, pp. 133–9

Simon, J.M. (1988) 'Humour and the older adult: implications for nursing', *Journal of Advanced Nursing*, Vol. 13, No. 4, pp. 441–6

Spiers, N., Jagger, C. and Clarke, M. (1996) 'Physical function and perceived health: cohort differences and interrelationships in older people', *Journals of Gerontology, Series B, Psychological Sciences and Social Sciences*, Vol. 51B, No. 5, pp. S226–33

Stevens, N. (2001) 'Combating loneliness: a friendship enrichment programme for older women', *Ageing and Society*, Vol. 21, pp. 183–202

Strawbridge, W.J., Cohen, R.D., Shema, S.J. and Kaplan, G.A. (1996) 'Successful aging: predictors and associated activities', *American Journal of Epidemiology*, Vol. 144, No. 2, pp. 135–41

Strumpf, N.E. (1987) 'Probing the temporal world of the elderly', *International Journal of Nursing Studies*, Vol. 24, No. 3, pp. 201–14

Tuohig, G.M. (1991) 'Health behaviors in elderly life-styles', the University of Utah, PhD

Vetter, N.J., Lewis, P.A. and Charny, M. (1991) 'Health, fatalism and age in relation to lifestyle', *Health Visitor*, Vol. 64, No. 6, pp. 191–4

Waymack, M.H. (2001) '"Busyness" vs. disengagement and the rhetoric of successful aging', *Aging Today*, Vol. 22, No. 4, p. 3

Wenger, G.C. (1997) 'Social networks and the prediction of elderly peole at risk', *Aging and Mental Health*, Vol. 1, No. 4, pp. 311–20

Wenger, C.G. and Burholt, V. (2001) 'Differences over time in older people's relationships with children, grandchildren, nieces and nephews in rural North Wales', *Ageing and Society*, Vol. 21, No. 5, pp. 567–90

APPENDIX: MAPPING OF SEARCH TERMS ACROSS DATABASES

See overleaf.

Set	Search term	Database and date searched						
		PubMED (27.8.02)	AMED (27.8.02)	CINAHL, 1982-97 (27.8.02)	CINAHL, 1998-2002 (27.8.02)	Cochrane Controlled Trials, 2nd qtr 2002 (27.08.02)	Cochrane systematic reviews database (27.08.02)	Combined (27.8.02)
1	Older people	66,164	379	636	1,367	282	60	2,724
2	Elderly people	886,556	418	677	590	349	49	2,083
3	Geriatric	884,659	617	1,715	1,294	1,442	66	5,203
4	Geriatrics	5,267	200	372	425	193	10	1,200
5	Retired	3,861	36	114	120	37	12	319
6	Retirement	4,356	83	527	563	58	13	1,244
7	Senior citizen	128	3	21	16	8	0	48
8	Senior citizens	380	22	59	59	14	0	154
9	Pensioner	32	1	2	4	1	0	8
10	Pensioners	158	4	9	9	6	2	30
11	1–10 (or)	916,096	1,584	40,937	4,120	2,147	145	11,908
12	Health	508,882	21,310	47,787	49,265	16,302	1,682	136,436
13	Healthy	164,272	2,610	3,899	5,102	26,832	323	38,766
14	Well-being	746	67	89	227	220	70	673
15	Wellness	70,677	149	859	700	63	7	1,778
16	Quality of life	65,699	2,893	3,679	4,891	4,806	868	17,137
17	Happiness	1,315	63	129	154	83	4	433
18	12–17 (or)	683,883	25,193	53,777	56,529	45,729	1,939	183,154
19	Belief	84,607	278	982	780	388	106	2,534

Continued

Set	Search term	Database and date searched						
		PubMED (27.8.02)	AMED (27.8.02)	CINAHL, 1982–97 (27.8.02)	CINAHL, 1998–2002 (27.8.02)	Cochrane Controlled Trials, 2nd qtr 2002 (27.08.02)	Cochrane systematic reviews database (27.08.02)	Combined (27.8.02)
20	Beliefs	85,605	504	2,066	1,690	459	91	4,810
21	Model	169,303	4,587	10,375	8,452	7,042	1,194	31,650
22	Models	243,584	4,088	3,280	3,300	6,451	471	17,590
23	Definition	20,905	474	1,325	1,255	686	733	4,473
24	Definitions	7,007	246	787	905	199	373	251
25	Perception	111,728	1,739	3,267	2,393	3,958	182	11,797
26	Perceptions	111,118	1,006	4,130	3,137	735	77	9,085
27	Meaning	8,158	516	1,709	1,385	255	90	3,955
28	Meanings	1,891	100	482	404	31	6	992
29	19–28 (or)	552,534	10,827	22,954	19,978	17,280	1,834	73,093
30	Healthy ageing	6,023	9	4	16	0	0	29
31	Healthy aging	6,708	6	50	27	6	1	90
32	Active ageing	1,478	0	0	2	0	0	2
33	Active aging	1,898	1	2	1	1	0	5
34	Successful ageing	566	8	5	11	1	1	26
35	Successful aging	790	14	28	40	3	0	85
36	Comfortable ageing	38	0	0	0	0	0	0
37	Comfortable aging	44	0	0	0	0	0	0

Continued

Set	Search term	Database and date searched						
		PubMED (27.8.02)	AMED (27.8.02)	CINAHL, 1982–97 (27.8.02)	CINAHL, 1998–2002 (27.8.02)	Cochrane Controlled Trials, 2nd qtr 2002 (27.08.02)	Cochrane systematic reviews database (27.08.02)	Combined (27.8.02)
38	Optimal ageing	447	0	0	0	0	0	0
39	Optimal aging	573	0	0	1	0	0	1
40	Positive ageing	2,555	1	2	0	0	0	3
41	Positive aging	3,134	0	0	1	2	0	3
42	Healthy longevity	199	0	0	0	0	0	0
43	Healthy and productive ageing	16	0	0	0	0	0	0
44	Healthy and productive aging	16	0	0	0	0	0	0
45	Healthy life style	1,246	1	11	8	2	0	22
46	30–45 (or) 38–53 (or)	13,473	40	102	105	15	2	261
47	11 and 18 and 29	25,116	112	223	245	125	127	832
48	46 or 47	37,547	149	322	344	138	129	1,080

Notes:

An additional search was carried out on the topic 'older people and adaptation' in December 2002.

Combined search across AMED, CINAHL and Cochrane Systematic Reviews retrieved 28 references.

Search on Medline retrieved 1,433 references.

'or' is used as a search term to find items using all of the terms in the sets indicated.